# Sparks May Fly

# Sparks May Fly

Jason J. Humphreys

To my darling wife, Becky.
Thank you for bringing light
into my dark.

# Contents

# Sparks May Fly

a crackling...
the hearing enters before seeing
all of its vibrant vermilion splendour

a popping...
a snapping...
an explosion of dry corn kernels
without the corn

seminal views of a
glowing
rising
mesmerizing
hypnotizing
a bearing of us away
in visions of holy majesty
to the outermost existential
reaches

we can touch the sun's surface
without the burning
without the blindness

a captivating and
obliterating power
to cleanse
to heal
to draw us into its
inviting temperate caress

illusory thoughts convince us
we are the ones in control
we set the boundaries
we are the orchestrators
the lion tamers

in eager expectancy
we throw on one more

then another
then another
then another

we turn our backs in
inevitable blind trust
and it rushes the barn doors
past the fence

where did we go wrong?

it waited for its chance
biding its time
(stubborn creature)
and in our minds eye
what took hours to kindle
we are now scrambling
to smother
both in and out of hearth

we're ice cold
shivering uncontrollably
drenched in sweat
and smoke stink
eyes filled to overflowing
with distortions of half-drawn
charcoal sketches

we're the flashpoint
the blame sits squarely
on our shoulders

yes
conflagrations can be
hauntingly beautiful
magnificent even
but at what cost?

so with eyes that lock
minds that meet
souls that touch
that electrochemical

combination
there is a kindling
a stoking through
glances
stares
and Freudian slips

we were under the illusion
that we could handle the flame
and how we revelled in
those peculiar burning sensations
we are trained fire eaters
after all

nonetheless
we failed royally

we swallowed passion whole
but turned our backs on
compassion and love
for we thought all fire was
the same

now the damage spreads
beyond our ken
our boundaries
as mutual friends
cross the floor in
a transcontinental divide
a tirade of emotion
while the stench of that
smouldering destructive swathe
permeates our clothes
our very membrane

nothing is left to
commend us now
but the rising ash and
charcoal stumps of
the paradise we planted

our hearts are forever soured
by this painful and astringent vinegar
for we went nuclear in a moment
and the fallout will last for
centuries to come -
a beautiful ethereal
disaster

# Words

O what worlds
come from words!

for when we write
you exist
and when we speak
you dance
(twirling off the page)

you ripple outwards
and beyond
enveloping minds
evoking limitless
imagery

while forests, fields,
and other fancies arise
from a single flourish
and hearts burst forth
joyful confetti
with one resonant
syllable

O how I adore
the emerging patterns
of words!

for without these servants
our hands lose their strength
their grip
and our voices are taken
hostage

but we are an unshakable
eternal universe
bubbling over
foaming at the mouth
effervescing

composing a concoction
so potent
so dynamic
no bottle shall it contain

would you dare imagine
a wordless existence with
no book or song -
a monstrous introduction
for the babe in
the silent womb
save the beating heart?

no, these ideatic synchronies
aren't life rafts in the
seas of consciousness
to safeguard us until
we reach firmer soils

they are the ocean liners
forged to transport us
to multiple destinies

and since we are both
captain and passenger
we can choose to sail
first class
without incident
without injury
to ourselves or others

so let wise words
fly straight
fly true
to meet their mark

let words of calm
coddle and soothe
the restless turbulent souls
turning wolves into lambs

and let humble, loving words
make light shine out of
the darkness
forevermore

## Daisies and Rings

his grizzled fingers trembled
with the extra weight and
as he poured the pain whispered
a certain something to him -
what was it now?
he knew it not long ago
so he left more room for milk
(she never left the bag in this long)

as he half-heard the droning
from the old short wave
he sipped
sipped
and sipped some more
(never slurping – it really got
on her nerves)
then he slurped, chuckled, and
quickly scanned the room
(just in case)

it was Sunday morning
and he donned Sunday's best
not for church though
(she'd be so disappointed in him)
why give his devotion
to a Being whose servant
when asked said a vacancy
needed filling?
(either can't be true or
there is no divine one)

therefore his everlasting kingdom
would be her resting place
and that was where he would worship -
her and only her
("where you die I will die," she quoted)

the old Ford still had that unclaimed
power he never had use for
(still drove ten miles below the limit)
you never knew beauty in the fast lane

as he lumbered down the winding
poplar lined trail the rustling
applauded him -
a runner to his slow and steady finish

he brought as he always did
seven wild daisies from the
meadow behind their homestead
(wrapped in moist paper towel
like she taught him)
one for each of the six decades of
sweet companionship and
one to swallow up his grief
as he sought remembrance
(he couldn't put it behind her ear
anymore – the right one that is
'cause the left one stuck out a little)

now his crooked cane was his lone
help-meet (couldn't keep house or him
from overspending)
and it took three stiff and painful tries -

up
(down)
up
(down)
up -

and as if sleepwalking
he was there with her now
kneeling in wet grass
muddy Bostonians
(sorry, love...)

he emptied her fluted porcelain vase
(it needed tending with its

mildew-green growth)
replaced the flowers
brushed clippings off of her stone
and twirled his ring round and round
staring at its untwirling embedded twin
without finger or hand for it to adorn

with visions of the hauntingly beautiful
sinuous touch casually brushing crumbs
from his cold pale lips
his pulse quickened
his palms perspired
his pallor flushed
and his eyes welled up
viewing with distinct irritation
"here lies Cynthia
loving wife and friend
of Joseph"

here lies Cynthia?

pine box
coffin
the bones -
these don't define her

she was more
so much more that
his chest felt hollow
emptied of life
ambition
desire
hope

she was the dancing
in shadows on candlelit
stormy nights
she was the dusting of flour
on denim aprons baking bread
she was the patience of Job
looking after Maude
(that crotchety nose-in-the-air

know-it-all!)
she was the mother to all new
mothers able to soothe the most
colicky babe with a single loving gaze
she was the giddy twenty-something
splashing him with pond water
climbing every tree that she could
she was that delicate songbird
of a voice with lilting notes which
softened the hardest heads and
the roughest faces
she was the glorious birth and death
of every star ever known
brighter in spirit and joy than
a billion supernovae

she was his world
his universe
his everything

Epilogue:

the caretaker found
the crumpled man
the next morning
covered in dew with
one daisy
mangled in his left hand
while the other?
frozen in the state of having
put his ring on top of hers

and a note placed under
the fluted vase which read
"Please look after Maude.
I don't want her to worry.
- Joe"

# Chimera

our sights continue set
on mountains of gravel
for in climbing them
we slide back down
(snakes and ladders)
taking them along with us

the summit grows higher
and is a stake designed to
pierce our hearts letting our
"whens" and "what ifs"
gush out in crimson splendour

we scurry with dreaded abandon
while holding aloft our golden forks
eager to devour puff pastries filled
with golden syrup and empty calories

it's that wasting disease of
insatiable wanton greed
for that which devalues and
decays at the opening of the day

still sliding down these mountains
of gravel (as we eat it by the mouthful)
more and more we want yet can't have
since we're the enslaved and addicted
denying that we have a problem with
bigger is better
more is better
for we deserve it
we are worth it
and there's no need to wait
we can have it all
right now

the plastic in our pocket is
worth its weight in bold
ruination of people and
planet
as the greenback distraction
shoves morality off the podium
crushing its hand
stealing its life
and we join in brutality
nodding in approval
because we are next in line

**

placing our hope in this juggernaut
with a life of its own
we keep going back and forth
mixing one paint with another
and look! something newer
something grander by far
something which may save us
from ourselves

to this masterpiece we ask
"what should we do?
what side of the bed
should we sleep on?
how should we brush
our teeth?
do we eat meat or veggies
or do we stick a needle
in our arm and a tube
in our stomach and let you
take your best shot?"

and though poisoned we may be
we are supremely grateful for
showing us the way for how else
can we paint possessing as we do
worn out brushes and canvasses
used
reused
and reused

whitewashing them over
each time we try

effectively brainwashing ourselves
we say that this time we will
get it right
and that mountain of granite
we've etched in our minds' eye
while we either place a hand over
our hearts or raise palms to our eyes
handing it a gun saying we pledge
our lives and love to you alone -
we await your command

we yearn for peace yet glorify
the bloody gods of vengeance
apologizing each and every time
as our barbs latch on and snuff out
another fragile candlewick
rationalizing through formulation
of copious reasonings why it was moral
and righteous and good
just to mute our battered conscience
which is screaming itself hoarse
until it gets up from the table
puts on its coat and hat and
slams the door on its way out
never to be seen from or
heard from again

when will we ever learn
that theft of the absolute
right to rule over ourselves
has led to a ticking bomb
armed and ready
and all we do is sit and
admire the craftsmanship

it's like touching the sun
living in the depths
guzzling sulfuric acid
by the tumbler full and

expecting no harm to
befall us

the grand experiment has
run its course and sets an
eternal precedent

the debate is over
the facts are unassailable
the data has been compiled
collated and copied for posterity

hypothesis:
can humans successfully govern themselves?:
result:
they are unauthorized
they are incapable

\*\*\*
I am the unholy temptress weaving
truth, half-truth, and lie into a veil
for my father to blind the sighted
smother the fire
and keep every distorted matter
properly balanced
one against the other

observe the multitude of my creations
available to the lowest and the highest
bidders for my fancies and tastes are
expensive and varied

I am the mistress of darkness
swearing up and down before
the innocent and guileless
that I am only light
a teacher of all that is right
and good

look at my numerous letters
recommending me to you
from all of my paramours

my fleeting lovers
raw in power, influence,
and wealth

drink my wine
feast at my table
and I will promise you
the gates of heaven
paradise itself
that you will become one
with the eternal

it matters not how
I tell the tall tale
only that you serve
my scheming purpose
only that you believe
body and soul

dream with anxious care
as I wrap you in this
tapestry of deceit while
you sleep fitfully under
this quilt of treachery

and as I commit many acts
of thievery by defrauding you
of faith and hope
and love
the freedom you signed up for
tears off its smiling mask
revealing its ugly head -
a prison of the mind
gilded and everlasting

# Bloom

ah!

the newness of life
spring's promise
never ceasing to fail
or amaze

colours galore
none clashing

that struggle from the
high Arctic tundra to
the tip of Patagonia

the Siberian steppes and
the Himalayan foothills
all bespeak glory

fleeting beauty
a blip in time
burning into the
backs of our eyes

so like the resplendency
of youth
bursting forth with
abject joy and mirth
folly amidst follies
power bejewelled
with innocence

# Weep

kneeling
her mind screamed questions
to the higher void -
a pink mitten
torn
unravelling
threads tearing

prostrate
her thoughts screamed questions
to the higher void -
a shattered frame
a shattered marriage
a shattered heart

curled into balls
teens screams out questions
to the higher void -
mannequins with lifeless eyes
from ten minutes of madness

crouched against rain-soaked brick
his brain screamed fiery questions
to the higher void -
locked out of work
house
and life

lives lean on lives
together screaming vitriol
to the higher void -
charred
wiped clear off the map
a town no more

the One hearing answers back
without malice or deceit
with tears in His eyes

feeling the global pain -
"after all of this time
why won't you listen to me?"

# Poetica Iustitia

ever the unfulfilled
with a dark roast and
ledger bursting in hand
thus begins my day's
accountancy

each soul encountered
has a place in my book
and some to their credit
have no debt to speak of

I'm Anubis for the modern man
judge, jury, and assassin
wielding my pen deftly
against those who vex me

I don my powdered wig
whilst doffing compassion
for my inner elephant
never forgets

demanding satisfaction
quaffing vengeance like mead
I savour high notes of victory
leading to a bitter end

my iron tower is impermeable -
the safest and
loneliest
place on earth
and here is where
I sleep standing
(my ground)
replaying footage
(in case I missed any
justification)
over and over

look now!...
the collectors that I've
ignored far too long
surround my castle
with bursting ledgers
piled high in one hand
and scales tipping
in the other
and a mob of firebrands
to pay back Shylock's
things to Shylock

# Carefree

a little man
eyes agape
excitement welling up
from toes
a makeshift pond
"look, Daddy!...
a swamp!"

what happened to it all?
I'll tell you -
the ticking clock
the 9 to 5
the burden of beastly man
the stress of metal and stone

yearning for one
long-lasting mental reset
where can I chew as much
bubble gum as I want?
play in the mud
the only goal being to
have it squish between my toes
in my expensive shoes?
drift lazily for miles on end
down rivers swift and winding?

wonder of wonders
I form sandcastles
housing fair princesses
while knights courageous
and true
stave off fiery dragons

in a world too busy and
distracting for quiet minds
the freeways of insanity
crowd out scenic coastal routes
so that I can't mentally downshift

to pass the dull and deliberately
uninformed

now don't get me wrong...
I don't want to be out in front
taking the lead
or for others to
eat my dust
I just don't want to
eat theirs

for our minds are
so corrupt
so toxic
the very sun
blackens and bloats
raining down despair
each night
swallowing joy
by day

therefore know by these words
I seek your calm and peace
I seek good for that is what
I choose to share

since objects at rest tend to stay
at rest
minds at peace must tend to stay
at peace

until a new paradigm comes into play
I calm my storm by higher means
choosing to smooth out
the cluttered and bouldered road
and though winds roar around me
I choose to stand in its eye
looking inward
outward and
upward
all at the same time

# Song of the Trees

give me a tree
and I'll sing you a song
of rain-soaked pine
and seed-plucked cones

recall the melody?
the rests garnished
with arms and batons
calling to attention

the rustling crescendo
reaches a fever pitch
where you can't help
but sway
bending your back
out of joint in time
to the tune

O the thrill of
sweet tones on a
brain that hangs on
every note
vibrates with every octave
and we bow in respect
to them for gracing us
with their opus
bringing harmony out of
nothing

# Ethereal Dancing

rising
falling
floating
sinking

this atmospheric
undulation
this sinusoidal
wave breaking

where thunderheads
grow like mushrooms
in a field of ripe
electricity

the ionic air makes me
bristle
feeling pure energy
course through my body's
path

lightning's waltz
choreographed by
precise laws
precise timing
takes on a delicate
and dignified form
leading to functional
awareness of self
out of self

# Caretaker

entrusted with a gift
we became mudslingers
laughing off the destruction
we create while drunk with
silly ignorance

stacks belch out filth
angry hornets chew up forests
yet our semblance of apology
is supposed to kiss it all better

the beautiful bumblebee that crawls
and feeds for five seconds on each
chive blossom doesn't know why
it's so confused and why
it can't fly like it used to

its happy buzz turns into
interrupted radio chatter
but of course we pay no mind
since we heed the creed:
profit before principle

the octopus can't tell the difference
between ink and slick
corals think white trash is the new
tropic of cancer

let the faithful now testify:
"ignore it and it will go away"
and the gods of greed and vice
will smell a restful and putrid odour

how disposable the cup
how disposable the system
how disposable the person

the decay we promote feeds nothing
but our sordid desire for more
and we hide from our own sickness
hoping it will all go away

we've yet to learn that
we can't stand outside of
the circle
the web
the connection

for though we're at the top
of our game
if the pyramid crumbles
we all do

# Rooted

you have grown weak
for I taste your disbelief
like bad perfume or cologne
it precedes you when you enter

the bindweed you promote
strangles everything good and
fruitful that it touches while many
look at its flowers and state:
"O how pretty!"

I'll stay far away from you
thank you very much
bloated as you are with
your own philosophy
ignoring plain and simple truths

I will never move out of my place
no matter how much you desire it
though your fire, storm, and quake
draw up many plans against me

the rock -
that firm foundation
which I surround and which
surrounds me
towers over me
protectively
is my trust
my confidence
and I fear no longer

# I Am Not

I am not a child
but I revel in childish
fancies

I am not a dreamer
but I would end all
nightmares to make
all dreams come true

I am not a fighter
but I will fight for truth
exposing all lies and
deceptions

I am not famous
but my fame rests
in proclaiming the
highest glory

I am no lover
but love is the lesson
I learn each day

I am no talker
but I speak with
passion about all that
truly matters
all things substantial and good

I am no leader
but I take the lead
by following the appointed
head of every man

I am not perfect
but perfection in thought,
affection, word, and action
is what I seek

I am not human
for humanity is corrupted
but I desire godliness
not to feel superior
but to achieve acceptability

I am no friend to this world
for its end is very near
but my best friends are
friends of the new world
soon to come

are you?

# Curtain Call

Thanks very much for choosing to read this book! Did it move you from within? Did it cause sparks to fly? Did it stir strong emotion? Please be kind and leave a rating and review.

Kindest regards,
Jason J. Humphreys

# Other Books by Jason J. Humphreys

The River Down the Road: selected poems

on second thought

# The Nicholsville Laureate

Please feel free to follow me on:

Amazon: https://www.amazon.com/author/jasonjhumphreys

Goodreads: https://www.goodreads.com/Hummerjay

Blogger: https://thenicholsvillelaureate.blogspot.ca

Pinterest: https://www.pinterest.ca/hummerjay53

www.ingramcontent.com/pod-product-compliance
Lightning Source LLC
Chambersburg PA
CBHW021148020426
42331CB00005B/956